AuthorHouse™
1663 Liberty Drive
Bloomington, IN 47403
www.authorhouse.com
Phone: 1-800-839-8640

First published by AuthorHouse 4/13/2010

ISBN: 978-1-4490-9170-5 (sc)
ISBN: 978-1-4490-9171-2 (e)

Library of Congress Control Number: 2010903197

Printed in the United States of America
Bloomington, Indiana

THE ABSITE™ QUESTION REVIEW BOOK

QUESTION

REVIEW BOOK

BASIC SCIENCES EDITION

William M. Greenberg MD

authorHOUSE®

TABLE OF CONTENTS

CELL BIOLOGY

Which component of the cell membrane increases its fluidity?
Cholesterol

Are cells (+) or (-) compared to outside the cell?
Negative, due to the Na/K ATPase (3 Na out, 2 K in)

What is the MC intracellular anion?
Phosphorous.

What is the MC intracellular cation?
Potassium.

What are ABO blood type antigens?
Glycolipids.

What are HLA type antigens?
Glycoproteins.

Which phase of the cell cycle is the most variable?
G1.

Which phase of the cell cycle do growth factors affect?
G1.

What are the 4 phases of mitosis?
Prophase, Metaphase, Anaphase, and Telophase.

During which phase of mitosis do the chromosomes align?
Metaphase.

During which phase of mitosis do the chromosomes pull apart?
Anaphase.

How many membranes does the nucleus have?
Double membrane, the outer one being continuous with rough endoplasmic reticulum.

How many membranes does the nucleolus have?
None.

In which part of the cell do steroid hormones bind to their receptor?
Cytoplasm. Subsequently migrate to the nucleus to act as transcription factors.

In which part of the cell do thyroid hormones bind to their receptor?
Nucleus.

What are the 2 purines?
Guanine, and Adenine.

What are the 2 pyrimidines?
Cytosine and Thymidine (DNA), and Uracil (RNA).

What type of biochemical bond binds purines and pyrimidines?
Hydrogen bonds.

How many bonds binds Guanine and Cytosine?
~~Single~~ *3* hydrogen bond.

How many subunits do ribosomes have?
Two; a small and large subunit.

What are the products of glycolysis for each molecule of glucose?
2 ATP, and 2 Pyruvate.

In which part of mitochondria does the Krebs cycle occur?
Inner matrix.

What are the products of the Krebs cycle?
3 NADH, 1 $FADH_2$, 1 ATP, and 2 CO_2 for each Acetyl-CoA molecule (i.e. 2x for each Glucose molecule).

Can fats and lipids undergo gluconeogenesis?
No, because their breakdown product Acetyl-CoA cannot be converted to Pyruvate.

Can muscle lactate be converted into new glucose?
Yes, via the Cori cycle, where muscle lactate is brought to the liver, where it is converted to pyruvate, and subsequently undergoes gluconeogenesis to form glucose.

Which organelle produces proteins for export?
Rough endoplasmic reticulum.

Which organelle produces lipids/steroids?
Smooth endoplasmic reticulum.

Which organelle modifies export proteins?
Golgi apparatus.

Which protein activates Protein Kinase A?
cAMP.

Which proteins activates Protein Kinase C?
Diacylglycerol (DAG), and Calcium.

What is the intermediate filaments in muscle?
Desmin.

What is the intermediate filaments in fibroblasts?
Vimentin.

What is the intermediate filaments in hair/nails?
Keratin.

What type of cellular filaments are found in cilia, axons, and centrioles?
Microtubules.

FLUIDS/ELECTROLYTES

How much of the Total Body Water is intracellular?
2/3.

In which cells is most of the body's intracellular water?
Muscle.

What is the MCC of volume overload?
Iatrogenic.

What is responsible for the plasma-interstitial osmotic pressure gradient?
Proteins, mainly albumin.

What is responsible for the intracellular-extracellular pressure gradient?
Sodium.

How many mEq of Na^+ and Cl^- does a Liter of 0.9% normal saline contain?
154 mEq of each.

What are all the electrolytes in Lactated Ringer's?
Sodium, potassium, calcium, chloride, and bicarbonate.

How is plasma osmolarity calculated?
(2Na) x (Glucose/18) x (BUN/2.8).

How is free water deficit calculated?
0.6 x kg x [(Na/140) -1]

What drop in measured sodium does each 100 mg/dl rise in glucose cause?
3 mEq/L drop in measured sodium for every 100 mg/dl rise in glucose.

What is the effect of acidosis on serum calcium?
Acidosis promotes calcium dissociation from albumin. Acidosis therefore causes increased free/ionized calcium.

How much fluid is lost to evaporation in open abdominal cases?
Up to 1 L/hr.

How much fluid is lost to insensible fluid losses (seat, respiration, etc)?
Up to 10cc/kg/day.

What is the benefit to switching to dextrose containing IV fluids after GI surgery?
Dextrose will stimulate insulin release, and hence amino acid uptake and protein synthesis (prevent catabolism).

How many grams of dextrose does a Liter of D5W contain?
50g.

How much fluid is secreted by the stomach per day?
1-2 L/day.

How much fluid is secreted by each of pancreas, duodenum, and biliary system?
Each produce up to 1 L/day.

What are daily potassium requirements?
1 mEq/kg/day.

Which body fluid has the highest concentration of potassium?
Saliva.

What effect does increased flow have on pancreatic/biliary secretion?
Increased flow results in higher levels of bicarbonate in the secretion.

What is the best test to diagnose the cause of azotemia?
Fractional excretion of sodium (FeNa).

How is the fractional excretion of sodium calculated?
Urine Na/Cr divided by plasma Na/Cr.

What is the FeNa in prerenal azotemia?
<1%.

Whys is myoglobin toxic to renal cells?
Myoglobin gets converted to Ferrihemate in acidic environments, which in turn is toxic to renal cells.

Which electrolyte decreases in tumor lysis syndrome?
Calcium.

What is the treatment for tumor lysis syndrome?
IV fluids to dilute, allopurinol to decrease further uric acid production, and diuretics to decrease potassium and phosphorous.

Where does the synthesis of Vitamin D in the body begin?
The skin, from UV sunlight to form 7-dehydrocholesterol. Subsequently gets 25-OH in liver, followed by 1-OH in kidneys.

What is the initial treatment of hyperkalemia?
Calcium-gluconate to stabilize the heart.

What is the characteristic EKG finding of hyperkalemia?
Peaked T-wave.

What are the EKG findings of hypokalemia?
T-wave depression, U-wave, ST depression, and QT prolongation.

Hypokalemia that is refractory to replacement can be due to deficiency in which other electrolyte?
Magnesium.

What is the initial treatment for hyponatremia?
Water restriction.

What is the effect of aggressive hyponatremia correction?
Central pontine myelinosis.

How is sodium deficit calculated?
0.6 x kg x (140 – Na)

What is the MC malignant cause of hypercalcemia?
Breast cancer.

Which diuretic should be avoided in hypercalcemia?
Thiazides, since they promote calcium reabsorption.

How does magnesium affect calcium levels?
Magnesium is required for PTH function. Hypomagnesemia therefore results in hypocalcemia.

What is the EKG finding in hypocalcemia?
QT prolongation.

What is the effect of hypoalbuminemia on calcium levels?
Each 1g drop in serum albumin decreases the measured calcium by 0.8.

What is the Henderson-Hesselbach equation?
$pH = pK + \log [HCO_3/CO_2]$

HEMATOLOGY

What is the intrinsic pathway activated by?
Exposed collagen, prekallikrein, HMW kininogen, and Clotting Factor 12.

What is the extrinsic pathway activated by?
Tissue factor and Clotting Factor 7.

Which clotting factor is the convergence point of both extrinsic and intrinsic pathways?
Clotting factor 10.

Which clotting factor has the shortest half-life?
Clotting factor 7.

Which clotting factor is not made in the liver?
Clotting factor 8 (made in endothelium).

Which clotting factor crosses the placenta?
Clotting factor 8.

Activity of which clotting factor is lost in stored blood?
Clotting factors 5 and 8.

What are the Vitamin K dependant factors?
Clotting factors 2, 7, 9, 10, and Protein C and S.

Which clotting factor helps crosslink fibrin?
Clotting factor 13.

What does Protein C do?
Degrades clotting factor 5, 13, and fibrinogen.

Where is tissue plasminogen activator made?
Endothelium.

What is the half life of RBC's?
120 days.

What is the half life of platelets?
7 days.

What is the half life of PMN's?
1-2 days.

Where is Prostacyclin made, and what does it do?
From Endothelium, decreases platelet aggregation and promotes vasodilation.

Where is Thromboxane made, and what does it do?
From platelets, promotes platelet aggregation and vasoconstriction.

Which blood product has the highest concentration of clotting factor 8 and von Willebrand factor?
Cryoprecipitate.

Which blood product has the highest concentration of fibrinogen?
Cryoprecipitate.

What is the treatment of symptomatic hypofibrinogenemia?
Cryoprecipitate.

Which product stimulates release of clotting factor 8 and von Willebrand factor from the endothelium?
DDAVP and estrogens.

What is the best for liver synthetic function?
PT/INR.

What is the treatment for a first-time DVT? Second time? Third time?
Coumadin for 6 months, for 1 year, and for lifetime, respectively.

What is the MCC of surgical bleeding?
Incomplete hemostasis.

What is the MC congenital bleeding disorder?
Von Willebrand's disease.

What does von Willebrand factor do?
Helps link platelets to collagen (via platelet's GPIb receptor).

What disease is characterized by platelet GPIb receptor deficiency?
Bernard-Soulier.

What is the only autosomal dominant bleeding disorder?
Von Willebrand disease types 1 and 2.

What is the only autosomal dominant hypercoagulable disorder?
Antithrombin III deficiency.

How many types of von Willebrand's disease are there?
3.

What is the specific defect in von Willebrand's disease types 1 and 3?
Type 1 is characterized by decreased quantities of vWF, whereas type 3 is characterized by absent vWF.

What is the specific defect in von Willebrand's disease type 2?
Type 2 vWD is characterized by dysfunctional vWF.

DDAVP is NOT helpful in which type of von Willebrand disease?
Type 2; DDAVP stimulates vWF release from the endothelium, but if the vWF is dysfunctional, there is no benefit from stimulating vWF release.

Which type of von Willebrand disease is the only Autosomal Recessive type?
Type 3.

What is the method of inheritance of Hemophilia A and B?
X-linked recessive.

What is deficient in Hemophilia A? B?
Clotting factor 8 in Hemophilia A, clotting factor 9 in Hemophilia B.

What is the treatment of a hemophiliac joint?
Ice, range of motion exercises (keep the joint mobile), +/- cryoprecipitate. Do NOT aspirate joint.

What receptor do platelets use to bind to each other?
GPIIb/IIIa, via fibrin.

What disease is characterized by platelet GPIIa/IIIb deficiency?
Glanzmann's thrombocytopenia.

How does uremia cause platelet disorders?
Uremia inhibits platelet GPIb and GP IIa/IIIb receptors, as well as von Willebrand Factor.

What is the mechanism of action of Clopidogrel (Plavix)?
Platelet ADP receptor antagonist.

What is the pathophysiology of Heparin-induced thrombocytopenia (HIT)?
IgG Platelet-Factor 4 antibody.

Why is HIT sometimes also referred to as "HITT"?
The extra "T" refers to thrombosis, as HIT can cause platelet aggregation and thrombosis, forming white clots.

What is the treatment of HIT?
Stop Heparin as well as Low-Molecular-Weight Heparin, and anticoagulate with Argatroban or Hirudin.

What is the MCC of DIC?
Sepsis.

What is the MCC of DIC intraoperatively?
Blood product transfusion.

What is the treatment of DIC?
Treat of the underlying cause.

How does prostate surgery cause abnormal bleeding?
Prostate or ureteral surgeries cause abnormal bleeding by causing the release of Urokinase (which activates Plasminogen → Plasmin).

What drug inhibits Plasminogen's activation to Plasmin?
Aprotinin.

What drug inhibits Plasmin?
Aminocaproic acid.

What is the best way of predicting a patient's bleeding risk?
Thorough history and physical.

What is the MC congenital hypercoagulable disorder?
Factor 5 Leiden.

How does Factor 5 Leiden cause a hypercoagulable state?
In Factor 5 Leiden, there is a genetic mutation whereby clotting factor 5 becomes resistant to inhibition by Protein C.

What is the treatment for hyperhomocysteinemia?
Folic acid and B12, in order to drive the Methionine Synthase reaction towards Methionine.

How does "Prothrombin gene defect" cause a hypercoagulable state?
In prothrombin gene defect, a genetic mutation at position 20210A causes an increased amount of thrombin to circulate in the blood, thereby resulting in a thrombophilic state.

What is the method of inheritance of 'Antithrombin III deficiency'?
Autosomal Dominant.

Which type of blood product contains Antithrombin III?
FFP.

Which antibody is responsible for lupus anticoagulant?
Anti-phospholipid antibody.

Is lupus anticoagulant necessarily associated with SLE?
No, not every patient with lupus anticoagulant has SLE.

What happens to the PTT in lupus anticoagulant?
Despite causing a thrombogenic state, lupus anticoagulant causes a paradoxical increase in PTT. In fact, elevated PTT not corrected with FFP is indicative of lupus anticoagulant. ⚹ ⚹

What is the pathophysiologic etiology of venous thrombosis?
Virchow's triad: stasis, hypercoagulability, and endothelial injury.

What is the pathophysiologic etiology of arterial thrombosis?
Endothelial injury.

What is the mechanism of action of Warfarin?
Inhibits the Vitamin K dependant carboxylation of Glutamic acid residues.

What is the half life of Heparin?
60-90 minutes.

What can long-term Heparin cause?
Osteoporosis and alopecia.

Does Heparin cross the placenta?
No. Coumadin does.

How is Heparin reversed?
Protamine.

What is the MC reaction to Protamine?
Hypotension; occurs in ~5% of all patients who receive Protamine.

What is the mechanism of action of Argatroban?
Reversible direct thrombin inhibitor.

What is the mechanism of action of Hirudin?
Irreversible direct thrombin inhibitor.

What is the mechanism of action of Ancrod?
Stimulates Tissue Plasminogen Activator (tPA) release.

What are the 3 absolute contraindications to thrombolytic use?
Active internal bleeding, recent CVA <2 months, and intracranial pathology.

BLOOD PRODUCTS

What are the only 2 blood products that don't carry any risk of HIV or Hepatitis?
Albumin and Serum globulins.

For whom is CMV negative blood reserved for?
Low birthweight infants, and transplant patients.

What is the MC bacterial contaminate in blood products?
E. Coli.

What is the MC blood type to be contaminated?
Platelets.

Does stored blood have high or low affinity for O2?
Stored blood is low in 2,3-DPG, and therefore has a high affinity for O2.

What is the cause of acute hemolysis with transfusions?
Antibody-mediated.

How does acute hemolysis present clinically?
Back pain, chills, tachycardia, fever, hemoglobinuria. It can lead to ATN, DIC and shock.

What is the treatment for acute hemolysis?
IV fluids, diuretics, bicarbonate, Histamine-blockers, and vasopressors if patient is in shock.

What is the cause of delayed hemolysis with transfusions?
Also antibody-mediated.

What is the treatment for delayed hemolysis?
Observation if the patient is stable.

What is the MC type of transfusion reaction?
Febrile non-hemolytic reaction.

What is the cause of Febrile non-hemolytic transfusion reaction?
Recipient antibodies against donor leukocytes.

What is the cause of Transfusion-related acute lung injury (TRALI)?
Similar to febrile non-hemolytic transfusion reaction, TRALI is caused by recipient antibodies against donor leukocytes. But here, instead of simply getting a febrile reaction, clots develop in pulmonary capillaries.

What is the MCC of anaphylaxis with transfusions?
Recipient IgG antibodies against donor IgA's, in an IgA deficient recipient.

What is the MCC of hypocoagulability after massive transfusion?
Dilutional hypocalcemia (since Calcium is required in the clotting cascade).

IMMUNOLOGY

What are the 2 major interleukins released by helper T cells?
IL-2 and IL-4.

What does IL-2 do?
Stimulates maturation of cytotoxic T-cells.

What does IL-4 do?
Stimulates maturation of B-cells into Plasma cells.

Which cells contain MHC I?
All nucleated cells.

Which cells does MHC I bind to?
Cytotoxic T-cells (CD8).

Which cells contain MHC II?
Antigen-presenting cells, such as B-cells, Monocytes, Dendritic cells, and ~~Natural killer cells~~.

Which cells does MHC II bind to?
Helper T-cells (CD4).

Which cells are targeted by Natural killer cells?
Cells that lack self-MHC.

What is HLA-DR?
HLA-DR is a type of MHC 2. It is therefore only found on antigen presenting cells (macrophages, B-cells, dendritic cells, and natural killer cells, and presents antigens to helper T-cells (CD4 cells).

What are HLA-A/HLA-B/HLA-C?
HLA-A/B/C are types of MHC 1, and therefore present antigens from inside the cell to cytotoxic T-cells (CD8 cells).

What are opsonins?
Opsonins are products that fix complement, and therefore activate the classic complement pathway.

Which antibodies are opsonins?
IgG and IgM.

Which antibody crosses the placenta?
IgG.

Which antibody is the most abundant?
IgG.

Which region of antibodies recognized antigens?
Variable region.

What is the biochemical structure of antibodies?
2 heavy chains, 2 light chains, joined by a total of 4 disulfide bonds.

Which cell receptor does the HIV require to enter a cell?
CXCR4.

What is the major source of Histamine in the blood?
Basophils.

What is the major source of Histamine in tissues?
Mast cells.

What are primary lymphoid organs?
Primary lymphoid organs are involved in the formation and maturation of lymphocytes.

What are the two primary lymphoid organs?
Bone marrow and thymus, Liver

What are the two secondary lymphoid organs?
Spleen and lymph nodes.

Which antibody mediates type 1 hypersensitivity reactions?
IgE.

What is the series of events in type 1 hypersensitivity reaction?
IgE binds to antigen, which is then recognized by Eosinophils which have IgE receptors. Eosinophils subsequently release major basic protein, which causes Mast cells and Basophils to release Histamine, Bradykinin, and Serotonin.

Which antibodies mediate type 2 hypersensitivity reactions?
IgG and IgM, reacting to cell bound antigens.

What is type 3 hypersensitivity reaction due to?
Immune complexes, such as SLE or rheumatoid arthritis.

What is type 4 hypersensitivity due to?
Previously sensitized T-cells (which release cytokines, causing reaction).

When is tetanus toxoid ever given?

In any wound in patients with <3 doses of toxoid, >5 years since last booster, or status unknown.

When is tetanus immunoglobulin ever given?

Dirty wounds in patients not immunize, or status unknown.

INFLAMMATION AND CYTOKINES

Which factors are released by platelets in the inflammatory phase?
Platelet-derived growth factor (PDGF) and TGF-β.

Which gene codes for PDGF?
Sis oncogene; overexpressed in certain cancers.

What are the effects of TGF-β?
Chemotaxis and activation of PMN's, macrophages, and fibroblasts, as well as angiogenesis and epithelialization.

What can result from overproduction of TGF-β?
Fibrosis, hypertrophic scars, keloids.

What gene codes for the epidermal growth factor receptor (EGFR)?
Erb B (also known as Her2 and Neu) oncogene; overexpressed in certain cancers and carries worst prognosis in cancers when it is overexpressed. This receptor is blocked by the medication Herceptin (Trastuzumab).

What gene codes for platelet-derived growth factors?
SIS oncogene.

What is unique about platelet-activating factor?
Unlike other factors, PAF is not stored in cells, but rather cleaves off the cell membrane by phospholipases.

What is the precursor to Nitrous Oxide?
Arginine.

Which main enzyme is involved in nitrous oxide synthesis?
Nitrous oxide synthase.

What is Nitrous Oxide's biochemical effect on the cell?
Activation of guanylate cyclase, causing increased cGMP, and subsequently calcium sequestration (smooth muscle relaxation).

What is the other name for nitrous oxide?
Endothelium-derived relaxing factor (EDRF).

What does Endothelin cause?
Vascular smooth muscle constriction.

What are the 2 main cytokines in injuries/infection?
IL-1 and TNF-α.

What cell predominantly release IL-1 and TNF-α?
Macrophages.

Which cytokine is responsible for fever?
IL-1, by promoting PGE2 release, which raises the thermal set point in the hypothalamus.

What is the pathophysiology of fever in atelectasis?
Secretion of IL-1 by alveolar macrophages.

Which cytokine is responsible for cachexia?
TNF-α.

Which cytokine is the most potent stimulus for hepatic acute phase protein release?
IL-6.

Which 2 hepatic proteins are decreased in the acute phase response?
Albumin and transferrin.

Which cells predominantly release Interferons?
Lymphocytes.

What are the anti-inflammatory cytokines?
IL-4, 10, 13.

What activates the classic complement pathway?
Antibody-antigen complexes (IgG and IgM only, which is why IgG/IgM are called opsonins).

Which factors are only found in the classic complement pathway?
C1, C2, and C4.

What activates the alternate complement pathway?
Bacterial endotoxins.

Which factors are only found in the alternate complement pathway?
Factors B, D, and Properdin.

Which factor marks the convergence point of both classic and alternate complement pathways?
C3.

Which complement factors are chemotactic and anaphylatoxins?
C3 and C5.

Which complement factor initiates the membrane attack complex?
C5.

Which complement factors make up the membrane attack complex?
C5-C9.

Which electrolyte is required in the complement pathways?
Magnesium.

ASA inhibits which enzyme?
Cyclooxygenase.

All prostaglandins cause vasodilation except?
PGF2.

Steroids inhibit which enzyme?
Phospholipase (which converts phospholipids → arachidonic acid).

Which are the slow reacting substances of anaphylaxis?
Leukotrienes: LTC, LTD, and LTE.

Which platelet granules contain adenosine, serotonin, and calcium?
Dense granules.

Which platelet granules contain platelet-derived growth factor (PDGF) and TGF-β? *PF4, Thrombomodulin*
α-granules. *(?)*

When do catecholamines peak after injury?
24-48 hours.

What role does thyroid hormone play in tissue injury?
None.

What role do CXC chemokines play?
Chemotaxis, angiogenesis, and wound healing. *IL-8, PF4*

What does NADPH Oxidase do?
Produce Oxygen radicals from O_2.

In which disease is NADPH Oxidase absent?
Chronic granulomatous disease; resulting in an inability of phagocytes to kill ingested pathogens.

What does Superoxide Dismutase do?
Produce Hydrogen Peroxide (H_2O_2) from oxygen radicals.

What does Myeloperoxidase do?

Produce Hypochlorous acid (HOCl) from H_2O_2.

Which enzyme reduces H2O2?

Catalase reduces H_2O_2 to water and O_2. (+ Peroxidase)

With regards to cell adhesion, rolling is mediated by which leukocyte and endothelium receptors?

Rolling is mediated by binding of L-selectins on leukocytes to E-selectins on the endothelium.

With regards to cell adhesion, anchoring and diapedesis is mediated by which leukocyte and endothelium receptors?

Anchoring and diapedesis is mediated by binding of Integrins on leukocytes to ICAM on the endothelium.

WOUND HEALING

What is the first phase of wound healing, and how long does it last?
Inflammation, days 1-10.

Which cell type has the predominant role during the inflammation phase?
Macrophages.

Which is the first cell type to arrive in a wound?
Platelets.

Which cell type is most abundant during the first 2 days in a wound?
PMN's.

Which cell type is most abundant days 3-4 in a wound?
Macrophages.

Which cell type is most abundant days 5 and up in a wound?
Fibroblasts.

What is the second phase of wound healing, and how long does it last?
Proliferation, days 5-21.

What is the predominant cell type during the proliferation phase?
Fibroblasts.

What is the third phase of wound healing?
Remodeling/maturation, days 21-1 year.

When does neovascularization begin?
Proliferation phase.

When does collagen production begin?
Around day 7, during proliferation phase.

When does collagen production peak?
Around 21 days.

Which collagen type is predominant in early wound healing?
Collagen type 3.

What happens to collagen type 3 during the maturation phase?
My maturation phase/day 21, collagen type 3 has been completely replaced by collagen type 1.

When does collage type 1 synthesis begin?
Days 3-4.

What is the MC amino acid in collagen?
Proline.

Which collagen amino acids are required for cross-linking?
Hydroxyproline (hydroxylated proline) and hydroxylysine ((hydroxylated lysine).

What is required for the hydroxylation of proline?
Vitamin C, oxygen, iron, and α-ketoglutarate.

What is the MC type of collagen in the body?
Type 1 (skin, bone, tendons).

Where is collagen type 2 found?
Cartilage.

Where is collagen type 4 found?
Basement membrane.

Where is collagen type 5 found?
Cornea.

How long should we wait before revising a scar?
At least 1 year, to allow the scar to mature.

Which cell type is the last cell type to arrive at a wound?
Lymphocytes.

What is the main component of the extracellular matrix?
Collagen.

What is the most important factor in wound healing via primary intention?
Tensile strength, hence collagen deposition and cross-linking.

What is the most important factor in wound healing via secondary intention?
Epithelial integrity.

Which cell is involved in wound contraction?
Myofibroblasts.

How can we counteract the negative effects of steroids on wound healing?
Vitamin A.

How does radiation affect wound healing?
By impairing fibroblasts.

What is the difference between hypertrophic scars and keloids?
Collagen in Hypertrophic scars are limited to the confines of the scar.

What is the inheritance patter of keloids?
Autosomal dominant.

What growth factor is associated with hypertrophic scars and keloids?
TGF-β.

What are treatment options for keloids?
Pressure, steroids, silicone, and radiation.

What is the effect of bacteria on wound healing?
Decreasing oxygen content and collagen lysis.

What bacterial count is considered as wound infection?
$>10^5/cm^2$.

How do foreign bodies affect wound healing?
Retard granulation tissue formation.

What is the MCC of leg ulcers?
Venous insufficiency.

What is role of the nervous system on wound healing?
None.

NUTRITION

How many kCal are obtained from each gram of carbohydrate?
4 kCal/g.

How many kCal are obtained from each gram of protein?
4 kCal/g.

How many kCal are obtained from each gram of fat?
9 kCal/g.

What are the daily caloric requirements?
25 kCal/kg/day.

What are the daily protein requirements?
1 g/kg/day.

Approximately what percent of daily calories should be from fats?
1/3.

What does the Harris-Benedict equation calculate?
Basal energy expenditure.

What are the 4 components of the Harris-Benedict equation?
Weight, height, age, sex.

What is most of the body's energy expenditure used for?
Heat production.

How is the body's basal metabolic rate affected by the body's temperature?
Basal metabolic rate increases by 10% for each degree above 38 °C.

What are the daily caloric requirements in burn patients?
30 kCal/kg/day.

What are the protein requirements in burn patients?
An additional 3 g/kg for every percent area of body burnt. This is due to the high protein catabolism seen in burn patients.

What is the MC amino acid in the blood and tissues?
Glutamine.

What is the main source of nutrition for the small bowel?
Glutamine.

What is the main source of nutrition for cancer cells?
Glutamine.

What is the main source of nutrition for the large bowel?
Short chain fatty acids (namely Butyrate).

What is the main source of nutrition for the heart and muscles?
Fatty acids.

What is the main source of nutrition for the brain?
Glucose, but switches to ketones in late starvation.

Which cell types are the obligate Glucose users?
Nerve cells, RBC's, leukocytes, and the adrenal medulla.

What is the half-life of albumin?
20 days.

What is the half-life of prealbumin?
2 days.

How is the respiratory quotient calculated?
CO_2 produced divided by O_2 consumed = [CO_2 produced / O_2 consumed]

What is the respiratory quotient for pure carbohydrate metabolism?
1.

What is the respiratory quotient for pure fat metabolism?
0.7.

What is the respiratory quotient for pure protein metabolism?
0.8.

What is the main hormone responsible for the catabolic state seen on post-operative days 0-3?
Cortisol, which mobilizes proteins for gluconeogenesis, wound repair, and acute phase protein production. (Catecholamines and glucagon also play a role, but cortisol is the main hormone)

How many grams of protein contain 1 gram of Nitrogen?
6.25 grams of protein contain 1 gram of Nitrogen.

Which organ is responsible for amino acid breakdown?
The liver.

What is the name of the biochemical pathway in which amino acids are broken down in the liver?
Urea cycle.

How long do glycogen stores last during starvation?
24-36 hours.

Where are most of the body's glycogen stores?
Liver and skeletal muscle (mostly in skeletal muscle).

What are the main gluconeogenesis precursors?
Amino acids; specifically Alanine, from skeletal muscles. & Lactate, glyrerol, glutamine

What is the main source of energy during late starvation >1 week?
Fats and ketones, as protein utilization for gluconeogenesis slows down to conserve proteins.

What is the nutritional basis of TPN (total parenteral nutrition)?
Glucose.

What is the nutritional basis of PPN (peripheral parenteral nutrition)?
Fat.

What is the MCC of hypoglycemia?
Excessive insulin administration.

What is the second MCC of hypoglycemia?
Sudden discontinuation of TPN.

What is the effect of long-term NPO on enterocytes?
Having no enteral intake over a prolonged period of time Increases enterocyte permeability, and subsequent gut-bacterial translocation.

Apart from maintaining the integrity of the enterocytes, what is the other major benefit of enteral feeding?
Enteral feeding stimulates greater hormone release (insulin), and therefore promotes anabolism.

What 3 electrolytes are decreased in refeeding syndrome?
Potassium, phosphorous, and magnesium.

Which electrolyte does not decrease in refeeding syndrome?
Sodium.

Whys is refeeding syndrome such a potentially serious condition?
It can lead to cardiac arrhythmias due to the electrolyte abnormalities.

What is the effect of selenium deficiency?
Cardiomyopathy.

What is the effect of chromium deficiency?
Hyperglycemia.

What is the effect of zinc deficiency?
Alopecia and skin changes.

What is the effect of copper deficiency?
Pancytopenia.

What is the effect of vitamin E deficiency?
Neuropathy.

What is the effect of Niacin deficiency?
Pellagra (dermatitis, diarrhea, and dementia).

What is the method of absorption of short and medium chain fatty acids?
Simple diffusion into the portal venous system.

What is the method of absorption of long chain fatty acids?
Uptake by the enterocytes, where they form chylomicrons, and subsequently enter the lymphatic system.

Which organ clears serum chylomicrons?
Liver.

Which hepatic enzyme is required to clear serum chylomicrons?
Lipoprotein lipase.

In fat cells, which enzyme is responsible for breaking down intracellular triglycerides?
Hormone sensitive lipase breaks down intracellular triglycerides in fat cells, into fatty acids and glycerol. · sensitive to GH, catecholamines, glucocorticoids

What are the 2 essential fatty acids?
Linoleic acid (ω-6), and linolenic acid (ω-3).

What is the method of absorption of glucose and galactose?
Active secondary transport by Sodium ATPases (symport).

What is the method of absorption of fructose?
Facilitated diffusion.

What is lactose made of?
Glucose and galactose

What is sucrose made of?
Glucose and fructose.

What is maltose made of?
Glucose and glucose.

What is the method of absorption of amino acids?
Active secondary transport.

What enzyme activates trypsin?
The duodenal enzyme enterokinase activates trypsinogen to form trypsin.

What are the 3 branched-chained amino acids?
Leucine, Isoleucine, and Valine.

Where are branched-chain amino acids metabolized?
Muscle.

What are the 8 essential amino acids?
'*LIV Preciously Through The Magical Leopard*': Leucine, Isoleucine, Valine, Phenylalanine, Threonine, Tryptophan, Methionine, and Lysine.

INFECTION

What is the MCC of immune deficiency?
Malnutrition.

Which organism is most commonly responsible for gram-negative sepsis?
E. Coli.

Which endotoxin is most commonly responsible for sepsis?
Lipid A.

What is the role of endotoxin Lipid A in sepsis?
Lipid A causes release of TNF-α from macrophages.

Endotoxin lipid A is part of which component of gram-negative bacterial membranes?
Lipid A is part of the lipopolysaccharide (LPS) of gram-negative bacterial membranes.

What is the LPS receptor?
CD 14.

What is the other noteworthy portion of lipopolysaccharide (LPS)?
O-antigen polysaccharide side-chain, which is the major surface antigen of gram-negative bacteria, and therefore the major determinant of antigen-specificity.

Why do we get hyperglycemia just before a patient becomes clinical septic?
Due to impaired glucose utilization. ↓ insulin ↑ glucose

What is the MC bacteria in central line-related infections?
Staph ~~Aureus.~~ epidermidis

Which organisms are responsible for necrotizing infections seen just hours post-operatively?
β-hemolytic Streptococcus (Group A), and Clostridium Perfringens, due to exotoxins.

Which exotoxin is responsible for gas gangrene associated with Clostridium Perfringens?
α-toxin, a hemolytic lecithinase exotoxin.

What CBC and electrolyte abnormalities are typically associated with soft-tissue necrotizing infections?
WBC >20,000, and hyponatremia.

Which organism is responsible for Fournier's gangrene?
Fournier's gangrene is usually caused by mixed organisms.

What is the effect of Clostridium Difficile exotoxin?
Colitis.

What is the effect of Clostridium Botulinum exotoxin?
GI symptoms, diplopia, dysphagia, and paralysis.

What is the effect of Clostridium Tetani exotoxin?
Muscle rigidity/spasms.

What is the treatment of Clostridium Difficile infection?
Oral Flagyl or Vancomycin, or IV Flagyl.

What bacterial count is needed to diagnose a wound infection?
$>10^5$ bacteria.

What is the MC gram-negative bacteria in surgical wound infections?
E. Coli.

What is the MC organism overall in wound infections?
Staph Aureus.

What is the MC anaerobe in wound infections?
Bacteroides.

What is the MC non-surgical hospital infection?
Urinary tract infection.

What is the MC infectious cause of post-operative death?
Pneumonia.

What is the MC single organism in ICU pneumonia?
Staph Aureus.   #2 Pseudomonas

What is the MC class of organisms in ICU pneumonia?
Gram-negative organisms.

What should be suspected if a patient on appropriate anti-bacterials does not improve?
Fungal infection.

What is the treatment for a brown recluse spider bite?
Dapsone initially. May need local resection if large ulcer.

What are the MC organisms involved in septic arthritis?
Neisseria Gonorrhea, Staph Aureus, and Streptococcus.

What are the MC organisms involved in peritoneal-dialysis catheter infections?
Staph and Streptococcus.   *S. aureas + S. epidermidis

What is the treatment of peritoneal-dialysis catheter infections?
Intraperitoneal antibiotics. If there is peritonitis lasting more than 5 days, need to remove the catheter. (vanco + gentamicin)

What is the MCC of spontaneous bacterial peritonitis (SBP)?
Decreased host defenses, not transmucosal migration.

How is the diagnosis of SBP made?
PMN >500 cells/cc in the ascites fluid. Cultures of the ascites fluid are not sensitive, as they are often negative.

A decrease in which component of the ascites fluid is associated with increased risk for SBP?
Low ascites protein content <1g/dl is associated with an increased risk for SBP.

What is the next step in SBP that does not improve despite antibiotic therapy?
Look for a source of infection (secondary bacterial peritonitis), such as an abscess or bowel perforation.

What is the MC sequelae of hepatitis C infection?
Chronic hepatitis in 60% of patients, followed by cirrhosis in 15% of patients, and lastly hepatocellular carcinoma in 1-5% of patients.

When does seroconversion after HIV exposure occur?
1-3 months post-exposure.

Which medications decrease the risk of seroconversion, and when should they be given?
AZT and Lamivudine decrease the risk of seroconversion, but need to be given within 1-2 hours post-exposure.

What is the MCC for laparotomy in HIV patients?
Opportunistic infections (CMV most common), followed by neoplastic disease (gastric lymphoma most common). (NHL; 70% B cell)
followed by rectum

What are the most common causes of upper GI bleed in HIV patients?
Gastric lymphoma and Kaposi's sarcoma.

What are the most common causes of lower GI bleed in HIV patients?
CMV colitis and rectal lymphoma. , bacterial, HSV

When should PCP prophylaxis be started in HIV patients?
CD4 count <200, or in the presence of oral thrush.

What medications are given for PCP prophylaxis?
Oral bactrim, or aerosolized pentamidine in patients with sulfa allergies.

What is the MC organism in human bites?
Eikenella. — permanent joint injury

What is the MC organism in cat and dog bites?
Pasteurella Multocida.

ONCOLOGY

What is the MCC of cancer-related death in the U.S.?
Lung cancer.

Do T-cells require the MHC complex to attack tumor cells?
Yes. T-cells need the MHC complex to attack tumor cells.

Do Natural killer cells require the MHC complex to attack tumor cells?
No. Natural killer cells can independently attack tumor cells.

When are tumor antigens not random?
Tumor antigens are usually random, unless they are viral-induced tumors.

What is the overall MC cancer in women?
Breast cancer.

What is the overall MC cancer in men?
Prostate cancer.

Which molecules do PET scans detect?
Fluorodeoxyglucose molecules.

What is the effect on prognosis in tumors infiltrated by lymphocytes?
Overall better prognosis in the presence of lymphocyte infiltration (especially in Melanoma).

Adoptive immunotherapy requires which interleukin?
IL-2, which leads to the proliferation of a lymphocyte subtype 'lymphokine-activated killer cells'.

For which type of leukemia is γ–INF approved?
Hairy cell leukemia.

CEA is a tumor marker for which type of cancer(s)?
Colon cancer.

AFP is a tumor marker for which type of cancer(s)?
Liver cancer.

CA-199 is a tumor marker for which type of cancer(s)?
Pancreatic cancer.

CA-125 is a tumor marker for which type of cancer(s)?
Ovarian cancer.

Do CEA levels decrease immediately after colon cancer resection?
No. The half life of CEA is ~18 days.

Neuron-specific enolase (NSE) is a tumor marker for which type of cancer(s)?
Small cell cancer and neuroblastoma.

Which 2 cancers are associated with the Epstein-Barr virus (EBV)?
Nasopharyngeal cancer and Burkitt's lymphoma.

How does radiation promote cancer initiation?
Via direct small DNA breaks, as well as indirect DNA damage via oxygen radicals.

Which phase of the cell cycle is most vulnerable to radiation?
Mitosis (M phase).

What are 3 reasons why radiation therapy intermittent?
To allow repair of normal cells, for oxygen to build up (promote oxygen radical formation), and to allow redistribution of cells through the cell cycle (allow more cells to get to the M-phase).

What are the 2 characteristic radiosensitive cancers?
Seminomas and lymphomas.

Do cell-cycle specific chemotherapies exhibit a linear killing response?
No. Cell cycle specific chemotherapies exhibit a plate in their killing response, because only a given number of cells at any given time are in the cell cycle. Only cell-cycle nonspecific chemotherapies exhibit a linear killing response.

What is the active metabolite of cyclophosphamide?
Acrolein.

What is the "antidote" to cyclophosphamide?
MESNA, because it inactivates acrolein.

What is the main side-effect cyclophosphamide?
Hemorrhagic cystitis.

What is the mechanism of action of methotrexate?
Blocks the enzyme DHFR, hence blocking THF synthesis, and in turn blocking DNA synthesis.

What is the "antidote" to methotrexate?
Folinic acid (also known as Leucovorin), because Folinic acid does not require DHFR to be converted to Folate.

What is the mechanism of action of 5-Fluorouracil (5-FU)?
Blocks the enzyme thymidylate synthase, hence blocking dTMP synthesis, and in turn blocking DNA synthesis.

Leucovorin ↑ toxicity of 5-FU

What is the main side-effect of Doxorubicin?
Cardiac toxicity.

What is the main side-effect of cyclosporine?
Nephrotoxicity.

What is the main side-effect of bleomycin and busulphan?
Pulmonary fibrosis.

What are the 2 main risks associated with Tamoxifen?
Blood clots (1%) and endometrial cancer (0.1%).

Which 3 chemotherapy medications cause the least bone marrow suppression?
Vincristine, bleomycin, cisplatin., busulfan

For chemotherapy mediated bone marrow suppression, what product can be given to help stimulate the bone marrow?
G-CSF.

G-CSF can cause Sweet's syndrome. What is Sweet's syndrome?
Acute febrile neutropenic dermatitis.

List 7 tumor suppressor genes?
P53, Rb, BCL, APC, DCC, BRCA, MSH-2.

cellcycle   cyto. adhesion   HNPCC mismatch repair
          skeleton

On which chromosome is the p53 gene located?
17.

On which chromosome is the Rb gene located?
13.

On which chromosome is the APC gene located?
5.

On which chromosome is the p53 gene located?
17.

What is the role of the BCL gene?
Apoptosis.

What is the role of the MSH-2 gene?
Involved in DNA mismatch repair.

Which condition is a mutation in the MSH-2 gene associated with?
Lynch syndrome (hereditary non-polyposis colon cancer).

List 7 oncogenes? src?
Myc, k-ras, sis, Erb B, srs, Ret.

Erb B is also known as what 2 other names?
Her 2 and Neu.

What does the Erb B oncogene code for?
Epidermal growth factor receptor.

What chemotherapy medication blocks the epidermal growth factor receptor?
Herceptin (Trastuzumab).

What does the sis oncogene code for?
Platelet-derived growth factor.

What 2 types of cancers is k-ras most commonly associated with?
Colon and pancreatic cancer.

What does the Ret oncogene code for?
Tyrosine kinase receptor.

What cancer is most commonly associated with the Ret oncogene?
Medullary thyroid cancer.

What are the 5 genetic mutations associated with colon cancer?
APC, DDC, k-ras, p53, and MSH-2 (MSH-2 only in Lynch syndrome).

Mutation in which gene is the initial mutation in the development of colon cancer?
APC.

Li-Fraumeni is due to a mutation in which tumor suppressor gene?
p53.

What type of cancer is associated with naphthalene exposure?
Bladder cancer.

What type of cancer is associated with benzene exposure?
Leukemia.

What type of cancer is associated with vinyl chloride exposure?
Liver and lung cancers.

What is the MCC of axillary lymphadenopathy?
Lymphoma.

What is periumbilical node lymphadenopathy ("sister Mary Joseph's node) indicative of?
Pancreatic cancer.

What is the overall MC cancer to metastasize to the bone?
Breast cancer.

What is the MC cancer to metastasize to the small bowel?
Melanoma.

What is the MCC of malignant hypercalcemia?
Breast cancer with bone metastases.

In clinical trials, what is phase 1?
Figuring out whether a drug is safe and calculating the dosage.

In clinical trials, what is phase 2?
Figuring out if the drug is effective.

In clinical trials, what is phase 3?
Figuring out whether or not the drug is better than what is already available.

In clinical trials, what is phase 4?
The entire period after the drug is approved and release.

What is Krukenberg tumor?
Secondary ovarian cancer originating from the GI tract.

What characteristic histological finding is seen in Krukenberg tumor?
Mucin-secreting signet-ring cells.

What is the only tumor that is completely curable with chemotherapy?
Lymphoma.

What is Mycosis Fungoides?
Cutaneous T-cell lymphoma.

What characteristic histological finding is seen in Mycosis Fungoides?
Sézary cells.

What is the MCC of chylous ascites?
Lymphoma.

What characteristic cell type is seen in Hodgkin's lymphoma?
Reed-Sternberg cells.

What is the MC type of Hodgkin's lymphoma?
Nodular sclerosing type.

Which type of Hodgkin's lymphoma has the best prognosis?
Lymphocyte predominant type.

What are the 2 most successfully cure metastases with surgery?
Colon cancer to the liver, and sarcoma to the lungs.

In which 3 cases is the resection of a normal organ indicated to prevent cancer?
Colon in FAP.
Thyroid in RET + family history of MEN or thyroid cancer.
Breast in BRCA + family history.

PHARMACOLOGY & COMMON MEDICATIONS

What is the absorption of a topical medication based on?
Its lipid solubility.

What is the ED50?
The dose at which the desired effect occurs in 50% of patients.

What is the LD50?
The dose at which death occurs in 50% of patients.

What is the effect of Sulfa drugs on bilirubin?
Sulfa's displace unconjugated bilirubin from albumin. In newborns for example, this can lead to hyperbilirubinemia induced encephalopathy.

What is the difference between efficacy and potency?
Efficacy is the ability of a drug to get to the plateau. Potency is how fast it gets there.
↳ ability to achieve result w/o untoward effect   ↳ dose req'd for effect

What is tachyphylaxis?
Tachyphylaxis is the tolerance to a drug after administration of just a few doses.

What needs to be done if the peak of a drug is too high?
Decrease the dose.

What needs to be done if the trough of a drug is too high?
Decrease the dosing frequency.

What are examples of phase I metabolism reactions?
Simple demethylation, reduction/oxidation, hydrolysis.

What are examples of phase II metabolism reactions?
Glucuronidation and sulfation.

Which drugs are P450 inducers?
Alcohol, cigarettes, Phenobarbital, dilantin, theophylline, warfarin.

Which drugs are P450 inhibitors?
Cimetidine, allopurinol, calcium-channel blockers (verapamil, amiodarone), and antibiotics (erythromycin, isoniazid, ketoconazole, ciprofloxacin, metronidazole).

What is the effect of the P450 system on aromatic hydrocarbons?
The P450 system can transform aromatic hydrocarbons into carcinogens.

What is the mechanism of action of colchicine?
Binds cellular tubulin. ᵐⁱᵍʳᵃᵗⁱᵒⁿ ; anti inflammatory

What is the mechanism of action of allopurinol?
Xanthine Oxidase inhibitor, thereby blocking uric acid formation.

When used in gout, what is the mechanism of action of probenecid?
Increased renal secretion of uric acid.

What is the mechanism of action of statins?
HMG-CoA reductase inhibition.

What are the 2 main side-effects of statins?
Rhabdomyolysis and liver dysfunction.

What is the MC side-effect of Niacin?
Flushing. Can be treated with aspirin.

What is the mechanism of action of cholestyramine?
Sequesters bile acids, thereby inhibiting fat absorption.

What is the main side-effect of cholestyramine?
Decreased fat-soluble vitamin absorption. Can bind vit K + lead to bleeding tendency

What is the mechanism of action of promethazine (phenergan)?
Dopamine receptor blocker.

What is the mechanism of action of metoclopramide (raglan)?
Dopamine receptor blocker.

What is the mechanism of action of zofran?
Serotonin receptor blocker.

What is the mechanism of action of omeprazole?
Proton-pump inhibitor (blocks gastric H-K ATPase)

What is the mechanism of action of digoxin?
Na/K ATPase blocker, eventually resulting in increased calcium in myocardial cells.

What electrolyte abnormality potentiates the effects of digoxin?
Hypokalemia. can precipitate arrhythmia or AV block

What is the treatment of digoxin toxicity?
Digibind and potassium.

How does potassium help in the treatment of digoxin toxicity?
Depolarizes the myocyte membrane.

What are some side-effects of digoxin?
Yellow visual changes, fatigue, arrhythmias, and <u>mesenteric ischemia</u> due to decreased mesenteric blood flow.

Is digoxin cleared with dialysis?
No.

What class of drug is procainamide?
Class 1a antiarrhythmic.

What are some side-effects of procainamide?
Lupus-like symptoms, pulmonary fibrosis, QT prolongation, and torsades de pointes.

What is the treatment of torsades de pointes?
Magnesium.

What is the best single class of drug to reduce mortality in patients with CHF?
ACE inhibitors.

What is the best single class of drug to reduce the risk of MI and atrial fibrillation post-operatively?
β-blockers.

What is the mechanism of action of atropine?
Acetylcholine antagonist. ↑HR

What is the mechanism of action of vasopressin?
Acts on V1 receptors on vascular smooth wall, and cause constriction.

What is the mechanism of action of NSAIDs?
Cyclooxygenase inhibitors. (⊖ Prostaglandin synth → ↓mucus + HCO_3^- in stomach + ↑acid → ulcer)

What is the mechanism of action of Misoprostol?
PGE1 analogue, therefore promotes mucus production and hence prevent peptic ulcer disease.

What are the first symptoms of aspirin toxicity?
Tinnitus, headaches, nausea, vomiting.

What is the first physiological finding of aspirin toxicity?
Respiratory alkalosis.

What is the treatment of Tylenol overdose?
N-acetylcysteine.

ANTIBIOTICS

Which antibiotics inhibit the ribosome 30s subunit?
Tetracyclines, Aminoglycosides, and Linezolid.

Which antibiotics inhibit the ribosome 50s subunit?
Macrolides, Clindamycin, and Chloramphenicol. , Synercid
(Erythromycin)

All ribosome inhibitors are bacteriostatic except for which 2 antibiotics?
Aminoglycosides and Linezolid are bactericidal.

What is the mechanism of action of Ciprofloxacin?
DNA gyrase blocker.

What is the mechanism of action of Metronidazole?
Produces oxygen radicals that break up DNA.

What is the mechanism of action of Rifampin?
RNA polymerase inhibitor.

What is the mechanism of action of Sulfonamides?
Para-aminobenzoic acid (PABA) analogue, therefore blocking purine synthesis.

What is the mechanism of action of Trimethoprim?
DHFR blocker, thereby blocking THF synthesis and hence blocking purine synthesis.

What is the MC method of antibiotic resistance transfer between bacteria?
Transfer of plasmid.

What is the mechanism of Penicillin resistance?
Plasmid for β-lactamase.

What is the mechanism of MRSA/VRE resistance?
Mutation in cell-wall binding protein.

What is the mechanism of Gentamicin resistance?
Mutation leading to decreased active transport.

What added coverage do ampicillin/amoxicillin provide over penicillin?
Enterococcus coverage.

What type of antibiotics antagonize the effects of β-lactams?
?Bacteriostatic antibiotics.   Tetracyclines

Cefazolin needs to be given within how many hours of incision to be effective?
Within 2 hours of incision.

Why is cefazolin a good surgical prophylaxis antibiotic?
Good gram-positive, and long half life.

Which 5 antibiotics are effective against Enterococcus?
Ampicillin/amoxicillin, ticarcillin/piperacillin, vancomycin, aminoglycosides, and linezolid. , synercid

~~⊂ ampicillin~~
(β-lactams)

Tx VRE

Which 5 antibiotics are effective against Pseudomonas?
Ticarcillin/piperacillin, 3rd generation cephalosporins, aminoglycosides, carbapenems (meropenem/imipenem), and fluoroquinolones.

(resistance can develop)

Which 3 antibiotics are effective against anaerobes?
Metronidazole, clindamycin, and chloramphenicol.   Timentin/Zosyn , carbapenems

Which antibiotics are associated with a positive coomb's test?
1st generation cephalosporins.

Which antibiotics are associated with cholestasis?
Ceftriaxone and IV erythromycin.

↳ For CAP + atypical pneumonia

Which antibiotics lower the seizure threshold?
Carbapenems (meropenem/imipenem).

Which antibiotics are associated with Nephrotoxicity and ototoxicity?
Aminoglycosides and vancomycin.

Which antibiotic is associated with peripheral neuropathy?
Metronidazole.

Which antibiotic is associated with teeth discoloration in children?
Tetracyclines.

Which antibiotic is associated with pseudomembrane colitis?
Clindamycin.

Which antibiotic is associated with aplastic anemia?
Chloramphenicol.

What is the mechanism of action of acyclovir?
Inhibits DNA polymerase.

Which antiviral is used for CMV infections?
Ganciclovir.

Which antiviral is associated with bone marrow suppression and CNS toxicity?
Ganciclovir.

What is the mechanism of action of isoniazid?
Inhibits mycolic acid synthesis.

Which vitamin gets depleted as a result of isoniazid?
Vitamin B6.

What are the signs/symptoms of vitamin B6 deficiency?
Neuropathies.

What is the mechanism of action of rifampin?
Inhibits RNA polymerase.

What is the mechanism of action of pyrazinamide?
Inhibits bacterial fatty acid synthesis.

What is the mechanism of action of ethambutol?
Affects the mycobacterial cell wall.

Which antituberculosis medication is associated with GI symptoms (diarrhea, cramps)?
Rifampin.

Which antituberculosis medication is associated with retrobulbar neuritis?
Ethambutol.

All the antituberculosis medications are associated with hepatotoxicity EXCEPT?
Ethambutol.

What is the mechanism of action of amphotericin?
Binds cell wall sterols, thereby affecting membrane permeability.

What is the mechanism of action of fluconazole?
Inhibits the enzyme 14α-demthylase, a fungal CYP450 enzyme.

What is the antifungal of choice in suspected fungal sepsis?
Amphotericin.

Which antifungal is associated with Nephrotoxicity, fever, hypokalemia, hypotension, and anemia?
Amphotericin.

ANESTHESIA

What is the minimum alveolar concentration (MAC)?
The smallest concentration of an inhalation agent that is needed to achieve sedation.

How is lipid solubility related to the MAC?
More lipid soluble medications have a smaller MAC.

Does Nitrous oxide have a high or low MAC?
High MAC.

Which inhalational agent has the highest degree of cardiac depression and arrhythmias?
Halothane.

Which inhalational agent is associated with hepatitis (fever, eosinophilia, jaundice, elevated LFT's)?
Halothane.

Which inhalational agent can cause seizures?
Enflurane.

Which induction agent should be avoided in patients with egg allergies?
Propofol.

What is the mechanism of action of Ketamine?
Dissociation of the thalamic/limbic systems.

Which induction agent is contraindicated in patients with head injury?
Ketamine (due to increased cerebral blood flow caused by Ketamine).

Which induction agent is associated with hallucinations and catecholamine release?
Ketamine.

Continuous infusion of which induction agent can lead to adrenocortical suppression?
Etomidate.

Which induction agent does NOT cause cardio-respiratory depression?
Ketamine.

Which re the first muscles to be affected with paralytics?
Muscles of the face and neck.

What is the last muscle to be affected with paralytics?
Diaphragm.

What is the first muscle to recover from paralytics?
Diaphragm

Which are the last muscles to recover from paralytics?
Muscles of the face and neck.

Which induction agent has the least cardio-suppressive effects?
Etomidate.

What is the only clinically used depolarizing paralytic?
Succinylcholine.

What is the half-life of succinylcholine?
~5 minutes.

What can cause a prolonged paralysis with succinylcholine?
Decreased cholinesterase activity, seen mostly in Asians.

What is the first sign of malignant hyperthermia?
Increase in end-tidal CO_2.

What is the treatment of malignant hyperthermia?
Dantrolene (block calcium release), cooling, bicarbonate, and glucose.

What electrolyte abnormality is associated with succinylcholine?
Hyperkalemia. – depolarization release K^+

Succinylcholine is contraindicated in which patients?
Burn patients, spinal cord injury patients, renal failure patients, and trauma or brain injury patients.

What effect does succinylcholine have on glaucoma?
Can turn open-angle glaucoma into closed-angle glaucoma by causing striated muscle contractions in the eye, thereby increasing ocular pressures.

What is the mechanism of action of nondepolarizing paralytic agents?
Compete with Acetylcholine in neuromuscular junctions.

What is the effect of hypothermia on nondepolarizing paralytic agents?
Prolonged paralytic effect, because low temperatures affect Hoffman degradation.

What is the effect of hypercapnia/acidosis on nondepolarizing paralytic agents?
Prolonged paralytic effect, because acidosis affects Hoffman degradation.

Which nondepolarizing paralytic agents can be used in hepatic and renal failure?
cis-Atracurium, because it mainly undergoes Hoffman degradation.   -Histamine release

Which nondepolarizing paralytic agents has the shortest half-life?
Mivacurium.   Histamine release

Which nondepolarizing paralytic agents has the longest half-life?
Pancuronium.   MC SE - Tachycardia

Which nondepolarizing paralytic agents is eliminated by the liver?
Rocuronium.

Which nondepolarizing paralytic agents is eliminated by the kidneys?
Pancuronium.

How can we reverse the effects of nondepolarizing paralytic agents?
Acetylcholinesterase inhibitors (neostigmine and edrophonium).

What is the mechanism of action of local anesthetics?
Increase the action potential threshold, thereby prevent sodium influx and blocking the propagation of nerve/pain impulses.

What are the 2 main groups of local anesthetics?
Esters and amides.

Which is more allergenic, esters or amides?
Esters, because they are broken down to PABA, which is highly allergenic.

What is the maximum dose of lidocaine 1%?
0.5 cc/kg or 5 mg/kg.

Why are infected tissues hard to anesthetize?
Due to the acidosis.

Which local anesthetic has the longest length of action?
Bupivicaine. > lidocaine > procaine

In which body parts is lidocaine with epinephrine avoided?
In places with poor circulation, such as the penis, the ear, etc, because it can cause ischemia.

What is the first sign/symptom of lidocaine toxicity?
Tongue numbness/perioral paresthesias, followed by visual/hearing disturbances, muscle twitching, loss of consciousness, and seizures. Cardio-respiratory symptoms occur after neurological symptoms, and can include arrhythmias and cardiac arrest (usually V-Fib).

What is the mechanism of action of opioids narcotics?
Mu-receptor antagonists.

What is the 'antidote' to opioids?
Naloxone. (Narcan)

How are opioids eliminated?
Metabolized by the liver, and excreted by the kidneys. Toxic metabolites can therefore buildup in renal failure.

Why do we get papillary constriction with opioids?
Inhibition of the Edinger-Westphal nucleus in the brain.

Why do we sometimes get hypotension with opioids?
Some opioids can cause histamine release, which causes peripheral vasodilation.

Why do we sometimes get bradycardia with opioids?
Direct inhibition of the vagus nucleus in the medulla.

With which other class of medications should opioids be avoided?
MAO inhibitors, due to the risk of hyperpyrexic coma.

Why is fentanyl more potent than morphine?
It is more lipophilic.

What is the mechanism of action of benzodiazepines?
GABA-A receptor agonists.

What is the 'antidote' to benzodiazepines?
Flumazenil, a competitive GABA-A inhibitor.

What are the side-effects of flumazenil?
Seizures and arrhythmias (so avoid flumazenil in a patient with epilepsy or elevated ICP, because it might trigger a seizure).

Which benzodiazepine is contraindicated in pregnancy?
Midazolam (versed), because it crosses the placenta.

What is the etiology of post-spinal anesthesia headache?
Most commonly due to CSF leak form the puncture site in the dura, causing compensation of the loss of intracranial volume by vasodilation. It therefore presents with a dull headache, aggravated by sitting up.

How is post-spinal anesthesia headache treated?
Rest, increased fluids, and caffeine or theophylline to vasoconstrict intracerebral vessels. It is usually a self-limiting problem, but if it persists, a blood patch can be used at the puncture site.

In what kind of heart conditions are spinals and epidurals contraindicated?
Hypertrophic Cardiomyopathy and cyanotic heart disease, because spinals and epidurals can cause peripheral vasodilation, and patients with those cardiac problems cannot increase their cardiac output to overcome the hypotension caused by the peripheral vasodilation.

Why is fentanyl preferred in thoracic epidurals?
Because fentanyl has less cardiovascular side-effects than morphine.

What is the MC PACU complication?
Nausea/vomiting.

How far should an endotracheal tube be in relation to the carina?
2 cm above the carina.

What is the best way to confirm placement of an endotracheal tube?
End-tidal CO_2.

What is the MCC of a sudden drop in endotracheal CO2?
Most commonly due to disconnection from the ventilator. Although it can also be a PE or severe hypotension.

What is the MCC of a sudden rise in the endotracheal CO2?
Alveolar hypoventilation. Treat by increasing the tidal volume or respiratory rate.

CRITICAL CARE

Approximately what percent of the cardiac output do the kidneys receive?
25%.

Approximately what percent of the cardiac output does the brain receive?
15%.

What is the effect of the heart rate on cardiac output?
Cardiac output increases with increasing heart rate, but after ~150bpm , the cardiac output starts to decrease due to decreased diastolic filling time.

What is the effect of increased afterload on the contractility?
Increased afterload causes an automatic increase in contractility to try to overcome the increased afterload ('Anrep effect').

What is the effect of tachycardia on contractility?
Tachycardia causes an automatic increase in contractility ('Bowditch effect').

Which systolic pressure is higher, radial or aortic?
Radial, due to the difference in size.

What range is normal cardiac output?
4-8 L/min.

How is the mean arterial pressure (MAP) calculated?
Cardiac output x systemic vascular resistance = CO x SVR.

How is the ejection fraction calculated?
Stroke volume $\div$ EDV = SV/EDV.

Is the consumption of Oxygen by the body dependant of the oxygen supply?
No. Oxygen consumption by the body is generally independent of the Oxygen supply, unless very low levels are reached, then the body will start consuming less oxygen.

What is the effect of a "right-shit" in the oxygen-dissociation curve?
Hemoglobin has a decreased affinity for oxygen.

What is the effect of 2,3 DPG on the oxygen dissociation curve?
Right-shift.

What is the effect of acidosis on the oxygen dissociation curve?
Right-shift.

What is the effect of elevated CO2 levels on the oxygen dissociation curve?
Right-shift.

What is the effect of increased body temperature on the oxygen dissociation curve?
Right-shift.

What is p50?
The oxygen tension at SaO_2 of 50%.

What is normal p50?
~27 mmHg.

What is normal central venous pressure (CVP)?
~7 mmHg.

What is normal venous SaO2?
~70%.

What 3 things affect the mixed venous O2?
Hemoglobin, cardiac output, and tissue demand/extraction.

How does cardiac output decrease mixed venous O2?
Decrease in cardiac output will increase O_2 extraction from the capillaries and therefore decreased mixed venous O_2.

What is the effect of sepsis or hypothermia on mixed venous O2?
Sepsis and hypothermia cause a decrease in oxygen extraction by the tissues, and therefore causes an increased mixed venous O_2.

What is normal pulmonary capillary wedge pressure (PCWP)?
~11 mmHg.

What is the only method of measuring pulmonary vascular resistance?
Swan-Ganz catheter.

In which lung zone should a Swan-Ganz catheter be placed?
Zone 3 (lower lungs).

What should be done if hemoptysis results as a result of Swan-Ganz placement?
Pull the Swan-Ganz catheter a bit, inflate the balloon, and increase PEEP to tamponade the pulmonary artery bleed.

What are the main determinants of myocardial oxygen consumption?
Increased ventricular wall tension and heart rate.

Is there a pO2 difference between blood leaving the lungs and blood in the left atrium?
Yes, because bronchial veins drain into the pulmonary vein. There is therefore a small pO_2 drop between blood leaving the alveoli, and blood reaching the left atrium.

Which vessel carries blood with the lowest O2 saturation?
Coronary venous blood, due to the high myocardial oxygen extraction.

What is the cause of neurogenic shock?
Decreased sympathetic tone.

What is the treatment of neurogenic shock?
Fluid resuscitation, +/- vasopressors.

Hypotension that is unresponsive to fluids and pressors is indicative of what?
Adrenal insufficiency.

What is the next step in management of a Hypotensive patient unresponsive to fluids and pressors?
Steroid stress test.

Which steroid is the most potent?
Dexamethasone.

What is 'Beck's triad' in cardiac tamponade?
Hypotension, jugular venous distention, and muffled heart sounds.

What is the first echocardiogram finding of cardiac tamponade?
Impaired diastolic filling of the right atrium.

Which type of shock is the only type with increased cardiac output?
Septic shock (though severe septic shock with increased cardiac workload can lead to cardiogenic shock with decreased cardiac output).

Which 2 types of shock are the only types with increased systemic vascular resistance?
Cardiogenic and hemorrhagic.

Which is the only type of shock with increased CVP?
Cardiogenic.

What is the mechanism of action of activated protein C (Xigris) in sepsis?
Anti-inflammatory by blocking TNF production, as well as fibrinolytic.

Other than hypoxia, what are other possible signs of fat embolism?
Petechia and confusion.

What type of stain can in the sputum and urine can indicate fat embolism?
Sudan red stain.

Which signs/symptoms with pulmonary embolism carry a worse prognosis?
Shock, tachycardia, and tachypnea.

What is the treatment of pulmonary embolism and shock?
Thrombolytics or embolectomy.

What is the treatment of pulmonary embolism and right ventricular strain on echocardiogram?
Echocardiogram will most always show right ventricular strain in the setting of pulmonary embolism. Treatment should therefore be no different than any other case of pulmonary embolism, unless the patient is in shock.

When do intra-aortic balloon pumps inflate?
On diastole; triggered by the T-wave.

When do intra-aortic balloon pumps deflate?
On systole; triggered by P or Q wave.

When are intra-aortic balloon pumps useful?
Cardiogenic shock (MI, CABG)

How are intra-aortic balloon pumps useful?
They decrease the afterload, and improve coronary perfusion.

When are intra-aortic balloon pumps contraindicated?
Aortic regurgitation.

Where should the tip of the intra-aortic balloon pump catheter be?
Distal to the left subclavian.

What is the effect of dopamine at 0-5 µg/kg/min?
Dopamine receptors only, hence renal artery dilation.

What is the effect of dopamine at 6-10 µg/kg/min?
β-adrenergic receptor, hence increased heart rate and contractility.

What is the effect of dopamine at >10 µg/kg/min?
α-adrenergic receptor, hence vasoconstriction.

What is the effect of dobutamine at 5-15 µg/kg/min?
β-1 receptor, hence increased heart rate and contractility.

What is the effect of dobutamine at >15 μg/kg/min?
β-2 receptor, hence vasodilation.

What is the mechanism of action of milrinone?
PDE inhibitor, therefore causing an increase in cAMP, and hence increased calcium influx into cells and increased contractility.

What is the mechanism of phenylephrine?
A-1 agonist, hence vasoconstriction.

What is the effect of low dose norepinephrine?
β-1 agonist only.

What is the effect of high dose norepinephrine?
α and β-1 agonist.

What is the effect of low dose epinephrine?
β-1 and β-2 agonist. Due to the β-2, low dose epinephrine can actually cause hypotension.

What is the effect of high dose epinephrine?
α and β agonist.

What is the mechanism of action of isoproterenol?
β-1 and β-2 agonist. Basically the same effect as low-dose epinephrine.

What is the mechanism of action of vasopressin?
V-1 and V-2 receptor agonist.

What does the V-1 receptor do?
Vasoconstriction.

What does the V-2 receptor do?
Water reabsorption in the collecting ducts, as well as promote von Willebrand factor and clotting factor 8 release from the endothelium.

What is the mechanism of action of sodium nitroprusside (Nipride)?
Arterial and venous dilation.

What is the side-effect of high dose sodium nitroprusside?
Cyanide toxicity.

What is the treatment of cyanide toxicity?
Amyl nitrite initially, followed by sodium nitrite, and lastly sodium thiosulfate.

What is the side-effect of nitrites?
Methemoglobinemia (oxidized Fe^{+3} heme)

What is the treatment of methemoglobinemia?
Methylene blue.

What is the mechanism of action of nitroglycerin?
Venous dilation; it decreases the cardiac workload by decreasing the preload.

Why is the SaO2 not a reliable marker in carbon monoxide poisoning?
Pulse oxygen saturation readers cannot hemoglobin that is bound to oxygen from that bound to carbon monoxide. Carbon monoxide poisoning can therefore give a normal SaO_2 reading.

What is the treatment of carbon monoxide poisoning?
100% oxygen.

What is compliance?
Change in volume over change in pressure = Δ volume / Δ pressure

What happens to lung compliance in ARDS or pulmonary fibrosis?
Decreases.

Which part of the lungs have the highest V/Q ratio?
The upper lobes.

What are the FiO2, PEEP, RR, pO2, and pCO2 parameters for ventilator weaning?
FiO_2 <40 %, PEEP 5, RR <24, pO_2 >60, pCO_2 <50.

How does PEEP improve oxygenation>
Alveoli recruitment.

What factors increase the risk of barotrauma?
Peak lung pressures >50 for >12 hours, and plateau pressure >30..

What is functional residual capacity (FRC)?
Expiratory reserve volume + residual volume.

What is vital capacity (VC)?
Inspiratory reserve volume, tidal volume, and expiratory reserve volume.

What is the effect of obstructive lung diseases on FEV/FRC?
Decreases FEV/FRC; low FEV, and high FRC, so the ratio ends up being low.

What is the effect of restrictive lung diseases on FEV/FRC?
Increased FEV/FRC; all the lung volumes including FRC are decreased, and hence the ratio ends up being higher.

What is the MCC of ARDS?
Sepsis.

What is the PaO2:FiO2 requirement for the diagnosis of ARDS?
$PaO_2:FiO_2$ <200.

What is the pulmonary arterial wedge pressure (PAWP) requirement for the diagnosis of ARDS?
PAWP <18, because otherwise the bilateral pulmonary infiltrates could possibly be due to LVH.

How do we calculate the partial pressure of a gas?
(Barometric mmHg – water vapor mmHg) x % of the gas. So for oxygen for example; (760 – 47) x 0.21 = 150 mmHg.

What is Mendelson's syndrome?
Chemical pneumonitis from aspiration of gastric secretions. The pH of the aspirate is associated with the degree of damage; higher acidity causes more damage.

What is the MCC of atelectasis?
Bronchial obstruction.

What are risk factors for atelectasis?
COPD and obesity.

What is the best test to diagnose the cause of azotemia?
Fractional excretion of sodium (FeNa).

How is the fractional excretion of sodium calculated?
Urine Na/Cr divided by plasma Na/Cr.

What is urine Na^+ in prerenal azotemia?
<20.

What are 6 indications for dialysis?
Fluid overload, hyperkalemia, metabolic acidosis, uremic encephalopathy, uremic coagulopathy, and poisoning.

Which cells release renin?
Juxtaglomerular cells, in response to low blood pressure or by β-1 stimulation.

What does renin do?
Converts angiotensinogen to angiotensin I.

What does angiotensin converting enzyme (ACE) do?
Converts angiotensin I to angiotensin II.

What does angiotensin II do?
Stimulates aldosterone release, and also causes vasoconstriction.

Where is atrial natriuretic peptide released from?
Released from the atrial wall, in response to atrial distention.

What does atrial natriuretic peptide do?
Inhibits sodium and water reabsorption in the collecting ducts.

Which cells produce antidiuretic hormone (ADH)?
Supraoptic cells of the posterior pituitary.

What is the main stimulus for AHD release?
High serum osmolarity.

How do NSAIDs cause renal damage?
Inhibit prostaglandin synthesis, and therefore result in renal arteriole vasoconstriction.

What factors exclude the diagnosis of brain death?
Uremia, hypothermia, hypotension, sedation medications, and metabolic derangements.

What is carboxyhemoglobin?
Carbon monoxide bound to hemoglobin.

What levels are abnormal carboxyhemoglobin?
>10%, or >20% in smokers.

What is the treatment of diabetic ketoacidosis?
Insulin, potassium, IV fluids, bicarb to keep pH >7.2.

GASTROINTESTINAL HORMONES

Which 3 GI hormones are produced by the stomach?
Gastrin, somatostatin, and ghrelin.

In which part of the stomach is gastrin produced?
Antrum.

Is gastrin also produced anywhere other than the antrum?
Yes, the pancreas.

What 4 things stimulate the G-cells of the antrum to produce gastrin?
Vagus nerve (acetylcholine), alkali gastric content, calcium, and ethanol.

What does gastrin then do?
Gastrin acts on the parietal and chief cells, to promote HCl, intrinsic factor, and pepsinogen release.

Which pathway is used by gastrin upon binding to parietal cells?
PIP-DAG pathway, leading to increased intracellular calcium, which activates protein kinase C (PKC).

Which pathway is used by histamine upon binding to parietal cells?
cAMP pathway.

Which 4 conditions will give an increase in gastrin levels, as well as an increase in gastric acidity?
Gastrinoma, G-cell hyperplasia, retained antrum, and renal failure.

Which 4 conditions will give an increase in gastrin levels, but normal gastric acidity?
Post-vagotomy, chronic gastritis, pernicious anemia, and medical acid suppression.

Where are most gastrinomas located?
Head of the pancreas.

What is the effect of secretin on gastrin levels?
Secretin decreases gastrin levels.

What levels of gastrin are diagnostic for gastrinoma?
Gastrin levels >1000, or >200 after a secretin stimulation test.

What is the single best test for localizing a gastrinoma?
Somatostatin receptor scintigraphy.

What are symptoms of gastrinomas?
Ulcers and diarrhea. The diarrhea here is due to lipases broken down by the increased acidity.

What is the association between gastrin and calcitonin?
Gastrin triggers calcitonin release in medullary thyroid cancer.

What are the side-effects of vagotomy?
Decreased receptive relaxation, causing increased liquid emptying, as well as decreased solid emptying. Symptoms therefore most commonly include diarrhea, but also dumping syndrome.

How effective is dietary changes in control the dumping syndrome post-vagotomy?
Very effective.

What procedure increases emptying of solids?
Pyloroplasty.

What is the role of ghrelin?
Increases appetite.

Which 3 GI hormones are produced by the duodenum?
Gastric inhibitory peptide (GIP), CCK, and secretin.

Which cells produce GIP?
K-cells

What does GIP do?
Decrease gastrin release, decrease insulin release.

Which cells produced CCK?
I-cells.

What does CCK do?
Increase gallbladder contraction, relax sphincter of Oddi, increase pancreatic enzyme secretion.

Which cells produce secretin?
S-cells.

What does secretin do?
Increase pancreatic bicarb release.

Which 4 GI hormones are produced by the small bowel?
Motilin, bombesin (gastrin-releasing peptide), peptide YY, and enteroglucagon.

What does Motilin do?
Stimulate the migrating motor complex (MMC).

What are the 4 phases of the MMC?
Phase 1 → 4: quiescence, acceleration, peristalsis, deceleration.

What is the length of each MMC cycle?
90 minutes.

Which part of the GI tract does the MCC span?
Stomach to terminal ileum.

What does bombesin do?
Bombesin, also known as gastric-release peptide (GRP), increases gastrin secretion, motility, and enzyme secretions.

In which part of the small bowel is peptide YY made?
Terminal ileum.

What does peptide YY do?
Opposite effect of GRP; decreases gastrin secretion, motility and enzyme secretions.

Which cells produce enteroglucagon?
L-cells of the small bowel.

What does enteroglucagon do?
Increase insulin release in response to luminal glucose and fat.

What is the effect of enteroglucagon after small bowel resection?
Causes small bowel mucosal hypertrophy.

Which 4 hormones are made by the pancreas?
Insulin, Glucagon, vasoactive intestinal peptide (VIP), and pancreatic polypeptide.

Which cells produce insulin?
β-cells.

What is the MC islet cell tumor of the pancreas?
Insulinoma.

What are symptoms of insulinomas (aka Whipple's triad)?
Hypoglycemia, symptoms of hypoglycemia, and relief of symptoms after correction of hypoglycemia.

Where in the pancreas are insulinomas most commonly located?
They occur evenly throughout the pancreas.

Are insulinomas benign or malignant?
Most are benign.

What is the insulin to glucose ratio in insulinomas?
>0.4

Which cells produce glucagon?
α-cells.

What are the symptoms of glucagonomas?
Symptoms similar to diabetes mellitus, but also dermatitis (necrolytic migratory erythema).

How is the diagnosis of glucagonomas made?
Fasting glucagon level.

In which part of the pancreas are glucagonomas most commonly located?
Distal pancreas.

What does vasoactive intestinal peptide (VIP) do?
Increases intestinal secretions.

Are VIPomas confined to the pancreas?
No, they can occur extra-pancreatically, like in the thorax.

What are the symptoms of VIPomas (aka Verner-Morrison syndrome)?
Watery diarrhea.

What does pancreatic polypeptide do?
Decreases intestinal secretions.

What bile mainly made of?
Mostly bile salts, but also lecithin, and cholesterol.

How is bile concentrated in the gallbladder?
Active reabsorption of sodium, chloride, and therefore water which follows.

What is the approximate quantity of the body's bile pool?
5g.

Approximately how much bile do we lose daily?
0.5g, or 10% of the total bile pool.

How often is the bile pool recirculated?
Every 4 hours.

What are the primary bile acids?
Cholic acid, and Chenodeoxycholic acid.

Made in the USA
Lexington, KY
07 September 2011